The New Novello Choral Edition

MOZART

Requiem

For soprano, alto, tenor and
bass soli, SATB and orchestra

K.626

Edited and with a new completion by
DUNCAN DRUCE

Vocal Score

Order No: NOV 070529

NOVELLO PUBLISHING LIMITED
8/9 Frith Street, London W1V 5TZ

It is requested that on all concert notices and programmes acknowledgement is made to 'The New Novello Choral Edition'.

Orchestral material for both the Süssmayr and the Druce completions is available on hire from the Publisher.

German Translation of the Preface by Gundhild Lenz-Mulligan.
Deutsche Übersetzungen von Gundhild Lenz-Mulligan.

French Translation of the Preface by Frédérique Normand.
Préface traduite en français par Frédérique Normand.

Copyright 1993 Novello & Company Limited.

The Duncan Druce version is recorded on EMI CDC 754525 2 (CD); 754525 4 (MC)

Permission to reproduce from the Preface of this Edition must be obtained from the Publisher.

Die Erlaubnis, das Vorwort dieser Ausgabe oder Teile desselben zu reproduzieren, muß beim Verlag eingeholt werden.

La permission de reproduire partie ou totalité de la Préface de cette Edition doit être obtenue auprès de l'Editeur.

Cover illustration: Facsimile of page 2 of the autograph full score of the Requiem, showing the first choral entries. Manuscript Mus.Hs. 17.561, fol.1v, from the Music Collection of the Austrian National Library, Vienna. Reproduced by permission.

Umschlagsbild: Faksimile von Seite 2 der autographen vollständigen Partitur des Requiems. Abgebildet sind die ersten Choreinsätze. Wiedergabe mit Erlaubnis der Musiksammlung der Österreichischen National-bibliothek, Wien (Signatur Mus.Hs.17.561, fol.1v).

Couverture: Fac-similé de la deuxième page du manuscrit original du Requiem, montrant les premières entrées des choeurs. Reproduit avec la permission de la Bibliothèque Nationale d'Autriche, Vienne (Mus.Hs. 17.561, fol.1v).

CONTENTS   TABLE DES MATIERES   INHALT

Preface
    The Commissioning of the Requiem   v
    Süssmayr's Completion   v
    The Autograph Scores   vi
    This Edition   vi
    Rationale for the New Completion   viii

Préface
    La Commission du Requiem   x
    L'Achevement de l'Oeuvre par Süssmayr   x
    La Partition d'Origine   xi
    Cette Edition   xi
    Reflexion au Sujet de la Nouvelle Version   xiii

Vorwort
    Die Bestellung des Requiems   xv
    Süssmayr's Ergänzung   xv
    Die Handschriften   xvi
    Diese Ausgabe   xvi
    Prinzipien der Neuen Ausgabe   xviii

REQUIEM, K.626, completed by Franz Süssmayr, revised by Duncan Druce

No
1   INTROITUS: REQUIEM   1

    KYRIE   6

    SEQUENZ:

2   Dies Irae   12

3   Tuba Mirum   19

4   Rex Tremendae   24

5   Recordare   27

6   Confutatis Maledictis   36

7   Lacrimosa   41

    OFFERTORIUM:

8   Domine Jesu   45

9   Hostias   54

10   SANCTUS   62

11   BENEDICTUS   65

12   AGNUS DEI   72

    COMMUNIO:

13   Lux Aeterna   76

REQUIEM, K.626, completed by Duncan Druce

No

(1	INTROITUS: REQUIEM	1)
	(KYRIE	6)
	SEQUENZ:	
2	Dies Irae	87
3	Tuba Mirum	92
4	Rex Tremendae	96
5	Recordare	98
6	Confutatis Maledictis	105
7	Lacrimosa	109
7a	Amen	113
	OFFERTORIUM:	
8	Domine Jesu	119
9	Hostias	125
10	SANCTUS	130
11	BENEDICTUS	134
12	AGNUS DEI	143
	COMMUNIO:	
13	Lux Aeterna	148

NB The layout of bars and page numbers in the Süssmayr version corresponds exactly to that in Novello's previous edition, for ease of reference in rehearsal when both may be in use.

PREFACE

The story of the composition of Mozart's Requiem has a strange, fabulous quality that is entirely typical of the events of his life. Whether we are considering his amazing exploits and achievements as a youthful virtuoso and maestro, or the depth of his financial misfortunes in Vienna in the late 1780s, there is little that is mundane about the main biographical facts. It comes as no surprise, then, to find that these facts have often been coloured and embroidered, to enhance their emotional effect, and to create a legend about this most remarkable musician. The simple story of the genesis of the Requiem is in itself striking − that in the last weeks of his life Mozart was working on a Mass for the Dead, that this work was the result of an anonymous commission, and that the commissioner's envoy, in order to avoid giving an address, paid Mozart several unannounced visits, like a messenger from another world − this story can easily be filled out with portents and hints of the supernatural.

Even the account by Franz Niemetschek[1] (first published in 1798, based on information given by Mozart's widow Constanze, and later receiving 'official' approval by being incorporated into the Mozart biography by Constanze's second husband, Georg von Nissen), writes of the commissioner's agent appearing 'like a ghost', and Friedrich Rochlitz's[2] account goes much further in suggesting that the composer was possessed by a demoniac and feverish desire to complete the Requiem, and conscious of approaching doom.

THE COMMISSIONING OF THE REQUIEM

Mozart's Requiem was commissioned by Count Franz Walsegg-Stuppach (1763-1827) as a memorial for his wife, who had died in February 1791. The Count, a keen amateur cellist and flautist, had ambitions to be known as a composer too, and had actually composed 'a few trifles', according to Anton Herzog, his former employee and quartet-partner. Herzog's account[3], penned in 1839, was not published until 1964. In it, he describes how the Count, at chamber-music evenings in his house, would encourage those present to believe that the quartets being played from manuscript parts were his own compositions. Title pages of music formerly in his possession even have the name Walsegg substituted for the rightful composer's, Hoffmeister or Devienne. He sought to maintain the same deception too with regard to the Mozart Requiem. Even after it had been published he told Herzog (who didn't believe him) that he had been Mozart's pupil, had sent completed portions of 'his' Requiem to Mozart for approval but had only received them back after Mozart's death, so the legend grew that Mozart had composed the work. The 'ghostly' messenger was Dr Johann Nepomuk Sortschan, a Viennese lawyer and Walsegg's business representative.

SÜSSMAYR'S COMPLETION

Of greater moment than the strange origins of the Requiem is the known fact that Mozart did not live to complete it, and the probably insoluble problem of discovering exactly how much of the familiar version completed by Franz Süssmayr (1766-1803) is by Mozart. Süssmayr, in a letter dated 8 September 1800 to the Leipzig publishers Breitkopf & Härtel[4] claims:

i) That several composers were approached to complete the work before he took over the job.

ii) That he had played and sung through the completed portions with Mozart and frequently ('sehr oft') discussed the working out and instrumentation of the work with him.

iii) That the completion of the Lacrimosa and the Sanctus, Benedictus and Agnus Dei were his (Süssmayr's) own work ('ganz neu von mir verfertiget').

Süssmayr also gives a generally accurate picture of which portions of the score are preserved in Mozart's hand.

The surprising thing about this is: if Süssmayr had indeed discussed in detail the completion of the Requiem with Mozart, why was he not the first choice (see **The Autograph Scores**, below)? It would also, of course, be of great interest to discover the precise nature of any discussions between Mozart and Süssmayr (was Süssmayr exaggerating here?) and to learn whether the 'new' Süssmayr sections of the score were based on any written or verbal information from Mozart. Constanze, writing many years later[5], expressed her belief that Süssmayr had access to fragments ('Trümmer') that showed the material of the 'missing' movements. At this point she was concerned to defend the Requiem's authenticity from those attempting to expose it as a forgery, but she was at pains to stress her knowledge of Mozart's working methods, and the likelihood that sketches would have been written.

One such 'Trümm' has appeared in recent years[6]. This single sheet of paper has a sketch for *Die Zauberflöte* on one side, and on the other two short sketches for the Requiem: four bars of the Rex Tremendae, and a fugal exposition to the word 'Amen', intended to follow the Lacrimosa at the end of the Sequence. The latter was not used by Süssmayr, but there is the clear possibility that similar sketches for Sanctus, Osanna, Benedictus and Agnus Dei were used by him as the basis for his 'new' movements.

From Constanze too we learn (in her letter to Breitkopf of 27 March 1799) that the idea of repeating the Kyrie to form the last movement was not Süssmayr's own but suggested to him by Mozart just before his death.

THE AUTOGRAPH SCORES

The original scores of the Requiem are contained in two volumes, both now in the Musiksammlung of the Austrian Nationalbibliotek (Mus. Hs. 17.561 a and b)[7]. The first is the complete score that Constanze presented to Count Walsegg, containing Mozart's autograph manuscript of the Introit and Kyrie, the Introit completed by him, the Kyrie with trumpet and timpani parts in Süssmayr's hand, and the doubling parts for violins, viola, basset-horns and bassoons written by another Mozart pupil, Franz Jacob Freystädler (1761-1841). Freystädler made many elementary mistakes in writing the transposing parts for basset-horns. The rest of this score is entirely in Süssmayr's hand, with no differentiation between his own and Mozart's contributions. The second volume contains the incomplete draft score in Mozart's hand for the movements that form the Sequence (Dies Irae, Tuba Mirum, Rex Tremendae, Recordare, Confutatis and Lacrimosa) and the Offertorium (Domine Jesu and Hostias). For all these movements, except the Lacrimosa, where he only wrote down the first eight bars, Mozart provides a complete draft of the vocal parts and the instrumental bass; he carefully figures this in the Introit, Kyrie, Dies Irae, Confutatis, and part of the Domine Jesu. He has also provided quite a few pointers to the instrumentation, as follows:

Dies Irae
Bars 1-4, violins 1 and 2, viola; 5-10, violin 1; 19-31 (first beat) violin 1; 40 (middle)-57 violin 1; 65-8, violin 1.

Tuba Mirum
Bars 1-18, solo trombone; 44, violins 1 and 2; 45-62, violin 1.

Rex Tremendae
Bars 1-20, violin 1; 22, violin 1.

Recordare
Bars 1-7, basset-horns; 1-14 (first beat), violins 1 and 2, viola (Mozart wrote rests in bars 1-6); 34-8 (first note), violin 1; 52-3, violin 1, viola; 68-79, violin 1; 109-110, violins 1 and 2; 126-130, violins 1; 126-8, violin 2, viola.

Confutatis
Bars 7-12, violin 1; 17-40, violin 1; 26-9, basset-horns, bassoons; 38 (last beat)-40, violin 2.

Lacrimosa
Bars 1-2, violins 1 and 2, viola.

Domine Jesu
Bars 43 (third beat)-46 (first beat), violin 1; 67-71 (first beat), violins 1 and 2; 71-8, violin 1.

Hostias
Bars 1-2, violins 1 and 2, viola; 44-5, violins 1 and 2; 46-54, violin 1.

In the movements of the Sequence this score also contains the attempts made by Joseph Eybler to complete the scoring. Eybler (1765-1846), a composer who eventually became the Viennese Court Kapellmeister, seems to have been the first composer Constanze approached to complete the Requiem. Later, an attempt has been made, not always correctly, to distinguish Mozart's own writing from that of Eybler by means of pencil enclosures of Eybler's additions, the original sections being labelled 'Moz' or 'Mozart'. Of particular interest is Eybler's attempt, for two bars, at a continuation of the Lacrimosa.*

THIS EDITION

The New Novello Choral Edition presents two versions of the Mozart Requiem. The previous edition of the traditional version (completed by Süssmayr) has been revised so that it corresponds exactly with the Mozart/Süssmayr autograph score. Though in general Süssmayr copied Mozart's manuscript accurately, he did make some errors, and there are even occasional instances of a deliberate alteration of the Mozartian original. Here we have returned to Mozart. The new vocal score is designed so that it can be used alongside the previous Novello edition, with the same page layout and numbering. The keyboard reduction has, however, been revised so that it presents a more accurate picture of the orchestral setting.

Together with the Süssmayr completion this edition presents, as an alternative, my own completion of the Requiem. For those movements where Mozart composed the vocal parts, the alternative appears in the vocal score in the guise of a different keyboard reduction, where my completion of the instrumentation is sufficiently different from Süssmayr's to make this necessary. Those movements where the Mozartian original is vocally incomplete or non-existent, however (Lacrimosa, Amen, Sanctus, Benedictus and Agnus Dei), are set out in full. A few specific editorial problems merit a brief discussion here, as follows:

THE TROMBONES

In bar 7 of the Introit, the bar before the first chorus entry, Mozart marks an entry for trombones on the lower three chorus staves; the assumption is that they continue to play *colla parte* with alto, tenor and bass. Süssmayr only specifically indicates trombones in the Dies Irae, Tuba Mirum (an extension of Mozart's solo for tenor trombone at the start of the movement), Rex Tremendae, Confutatis, Lacrimosa, Domine Deus, Benedictus and Agnus Dei. When instrumental parts of the Requiem were first published

*It seems likely that Maximilian Stadler, too, had a hand in the Requiem's completion. The evidence that he drafted instrumental parts for the Domine Jesu and the Hostias is discussed in a recent article by Christoph Wolff[8].

(Vienna, 1812), *colla voce* parts for three trombones were also provided for the Introit, Kyrie, Sanctus and the Communio (Lux Aeterna). I have generally followed the lead of this edition, but adding *colla voce* parts for the ending of the first Osanna, not provided in the 1812 edition.

DYNAMICS

In the Hostias the first dynamic indication in Mozart's draft score is the *piano* on the third beat of bar 24 (Süssmayr provides a *forte* for his wind parts in bar 23, but nothing earlier). In the eighteenth century *forte* was the assumed dynamic, barring any contrary indication. Does this mean that the opening of the movement should be *forte*? I suspect that many present-day performers would be reluctant to start this movement loudly. Even Süssmayr, by writing *senza tromboni* at the start suggests a more delicate approach. It seems to me that in a situation like this it is up to the conductor to decide what, for her or him, is the most convincing approach.*

'SOLO' AND 'TUTTI'

In the Benedictus, Süssmayr marks the first two vocal entries (alto and soprano) 'solo', but when tenor and bass come in at bar 10 there is no indication of 'solo' or 'tutti'. Nor does he indicate anything later in the movement — not even for the Osanna. It seems at least a possibility that he intended bars 10-27, and from bar 33 onwards, to be performed by the chorus. This solution would, moreover, make sense of the rather heavy scoring, including trombones, especially noticeable in bars 10-18.

TEMPO

Mozart provided tempo indications only for the Introit, Kyrie, Dies Irae, Tuba Mirum and Confutatis. For the Rex Tremendae, *Adagio* has been suggested, on the analogy of the Gratias Agimus of the Mass in C minor. For the Recordare, I would suggest *Andante*. The nearest parallel I have found is Pamina's 'Tamino mein! O welch'ein Glück' from the second-act finale of *Die Zauberflöte*. *Larghetto* is suggested for the Lacrimosa (also for the Agnus Dei, for which Süssmayr provides no tempo indication). Süssmayr suggests *Andante con moto* for Domine Deus; *Allegro*, or *Allegro moderato* might be more credible (compare the Confitebor from the Vesprae Solennes de Confessore, K.339). Süssmayr's *Andante* for the Hostias is less open to question. I have also provided new metronome tempo suggestions. These should be seen as approximate — dependent on acoustics, size of choir and other considerations. Where early metronome marks for comparable movements

exist (the metronome came into use in the second decade of the nineteenth century) I have taken clues from them, for the 4/4 *Adagio* movements for instance.

SLURRING

In his autograph score, Mozart, following his usual practice in vocal music, indicates syllable divisions by means of slurs as well as through grouping of quavers and semiquavers. In this edition, such slurs are omitted, but it should be remembered that, for Mozart, the slur has a function as an indicator of phrasing as well as helping to show the underlay. Thus, the paired notes in the phrase 'Quantus tremor est futurus' (Dies Irae, bar 41 and subsequently) need to be phrased very strongly, but longer melismas, such as those in the Domine Jesu (bars 35-40) indicate a smooth well-sustained line. By contrast, the long melismas in the Kyrie are not slurred by Mozart, thus indicating a more articulated delivery. The few slurs in the vocal parts are confined to the places where Mozart's slurring pattern does not precisely follow the syllable division. In the 'Süssmayr' sections (from the Sanctus onwards) there are no vocal slurs. In his autograph score, Süssmayr is less consistent in adding slurs, and, where these don't conform to the syllable division, it is not easy to believe that a point of phrasing is intended.

THE ORGAN CONTINUO

Mozart clearly intended to provide a meticulously figured bass for the Requiem, following C.P.E. Bach's precept that 'nothing that is necessary and essential should be overlooked'[9]. He put in figuring for the first three sections (Introit, Kyrie† and Dies Irae), for bar 2 of the Rex Tremendae, for the Confutatis (from bar 26) and for bars 21-8 of the Domine Jesu. These figures can give us valuable clues in completing the orchestration, for example the 9th chords at bar 28 of the Domine Jesu, ignored by Süssmayr. Mozart specified in addition the participation of organ in the Recordare, Lacrimosa and Hostias, by writing 'organo e basso' in front of the bottom stave of the score. Organ is not specified for the Tuba Mirum. We may wonder whether this is an oversight; did Mozart perhaps intend the organ to play throughout the Requiem, except when 'senza organo' is specifically indicated? He does ask for organ in the Recordare, another solo movement with an unfigured bass. Present-day performers, however, may well feel that organ continuo contributes little to either movement and prefer to omit it. In view of the fact that the Recordare is the only movement where Mozart asks for organ and then gives no further instructions, could this 'organo e basso' be a mistake?

---

*I am indebted to Robert Levin for pointing out this problem.

†It has recently been pointed out by Paul Moseley[10] that, from bar 20 of the Kyrie (bar 68 in our edition) the figuring is in Süssmayr's hand.

Süssmayr, as well as copying Mozart's figures, adds figured bass to his continuation of the Lacrimosa, completes Mozart's figuring of the Domine Jesu (except for the last 7 bars) and provides figures for his versions of the Sanctus, Agnus Dei, and, somewhat sporadically, Benedictus. For my completion I have, following Mozart's probable lead in the Tuba Mirum, not required organ in the Benedictus, but have elsewhere added a figured bass (there is no figuring in this vocal score, but in the full score available on hire from Novello). I have also provided an organ continuo part (also on hire), realizing the figured bass, for the whole work. Following several modern editions (Bärenreiter's New Mozart Edition, for example) I have supplemented Mozart's and Süssmayr's figures by using the figuring found in the first edition of the instrumental parts of the Requiem (Vienna 1812).

I have kept my continuo part as simple as possible, again following a precept of C.P.E. Bach that a continuo accompaniment should above all be discreet.[11] Bach's *Versuch über die wahre Art das Clavier zu spielen* provides, in its section on accompaniment, the best contemporary guide for anyone wishing to make their own realization. My organ part should anyway just be regarded as a guide: depending on the instrument and registration used, on the number of performers, and on the acoustics of the church or hall, notes may be added or taken away to produce a better balance.

RATIONALE FOR THE NEW COMPLETION

Süssmayr's work on the Mozart Requiem is of two kinds: the completion of the instrumental setting where Mozart had already provided a complete draft of the vocal parts and bass line, and the compositional work we must assume he did in writing or completing the other sections. Whilst the work as a whole has proved to be one of Mozart's best loved and most admired, it has been clear ever since it was first published that it sometimes lacks the perfection of detail, the smooth craftsmanship, the imaginative relationship of subsidiary material to the whole that is so characteristic of Mozart's other mature masterpieces. Süssmayr's orchestration, often perfectly workmanlike, occasionally inept, rarely imaginative, may not often get in the way of Mozart's vision, but rarely enhances it. With regard to the sections for which Süssmayr claimed responsibility there are some graver defects: the perfunctory quality of the Osanna fugues and the harmonic stagnation in the central part of the Benedictus are two such disappointments. Yet the main ideas of all these sections, whether they stem from Mozart or were composed unaided by Süssmayr, seem to maintain very strongly the unity and character of the work. The question of which parts of these movements, if any, could have come from Mozart has been discussed many times, and with very different conclusions, by

Beyer[12], Blume[13], Handke[14], Marguerre[15], Maunder[16], Moseley and Wolff among others. I do not propose to enter this discussion here, except to observe how difficult it is to prove or disprove authorship on stylistic grounds. Süssmayr's completion, anyway, will always have a special status, because of its long history in performance and because it is the only one by a Viennese composer of the 1790s, one who, besides, was best placed to know Mozart's own intentions.

Anyone coming to the task of completing the Requiem today is faced with some severe problems. It is not possible to rely entirely on parallels with other works of Mozart; the unusual orchestration of the Requiem, and the lack of any comparable large-scale sacred work from his last years ensures this. If we value the intense life and individuality of even subsidiary details in Mozart's music, we shall anyway do him a disservice by merely repeating features culled from other music. Whilst remaining alive to the possibilities of any genuinely helpful parallels in other music by Mozart I have attempted in a more general way to place myself in the position of a Viennese composer of Mozart's time, trying to complete the grand design of the work in the most convincing way. For the Lacrimosa I began by following Joseph Eybler's attempt at a continuation and built a movement whose construction parallels that of the Dies Irae at the start of the Sequence. The Sanctus is an adaptation of the Süssmayr version. For the Benedictus I used the main thematic material of the traditional version (the opening phrase comes from Mozart anyway — it is found in K453b, the exercise book for Barbara Ployer[17]) and composed a new movement, following a variety of Mozartian models and hints. The Agnus Dei, by common consent the most convincing of the 'Süssmayr' movements, I have retained, as regards the vocal and basso parts, until its final section, but I have added a longer instrumental introduction to the Lux Aeterna*; it seemed important to me to reintroduce the atmosphere and material of the Introit in a more decisive way. For the fugal choruses to 'Amen' and 'Osanna' I used as models above all the fugal pieces in the Requiem completed by Mozart — the Kyrie and Quam Olim Abrahae sections — plus the Cum Sancto Spiritu of the Mass in C Minor K427 and instrumental fugues such as that in C Minor K426. The starting point for the Amen was the short autograph sketch referred to above; for the Osanna I used the subject of the Süssmayr version. With the Amen and this more extended Osanna added to the other large-scale choral movements, the choral bias of the whole work, with its impressive, deliberately archaic contrapuntal features, becomes even clearer.

*This has presented a problem of bar numbering. In the Süssmayr version, Agnus Dei and Communio are numbered together; for the new completion the Agnus Dei and the first 6 bars of the Lux Aeterna are numbered separately, 'rejoining' the Süssmayr numbering at bar 53.

Several new versions of Mozart's Requiem have been made in recent years[18], each with its own viewpoint regarding the most necessary 'improvements'. These clearly reflect the current high level of interest in Mozart's music, and seem to me to be a very healthy sign. The Requiem is above all the major work of Mozart for which no definitive version exists. We can learn most from it, and be most inspired by it, if we experience it from different directions. Some aspects of Mozart's vision will have been obscured by one completion and enhanced by another. In 1814 E.T.A. Hoffmann was already strongly aware of the Requiem's qualities when he wrote that 'the music remains devotional throughout; pure devotion resonates through these awe-inspiring chords which speak of another world, and which in their singular dignity and power are themselves another world'.[19]

DUNCAN DRUCE, Holmbridge, June 1992

Notes

1) Niemetschek, Franz Xaver. *Leben des k.k. Kapellmeisters Wolfgang Gottlieb Mozart* (Prague 1798), translated Helen Mautner, London 1956.

2) Rochlitz, Friedrich. 'Verbürgte Anekdoten aus Wolfgang Gottlieb Mozarts Leben', *Allgemeine Musikalische Zeitung*, Leipzig, Oct-Dec. 1798. The relevant passage about the Requiem appears, in translation, in Robbins Landon, H.C.: *Mozart's Last Year*, pp.74-5, London, Thames and Hudson, 1988.

3) Herzog, Anton: *Wahre und ausführliche Geschichte des Requiem von W.A. Mozart.* Translation published in Deutsch, O.E.: *Mozart, a Documentary Biography*, pp.551-5, London, A. & C. Black, 1965. Also quoted in Robbins Landon, H.C., pp.76-82 (see note 2).

4) Translation published in the Introduction (by Günther Brosche) to the Bärenreiter facsimile edition of the Requiem autograph scores, Kassel, 1990.

5) Letter to Maximilian Stadler dated 14.3.1827. Bauer, A. and Deutsch, O.E. (ed.): *Mozart: Briefe und Aufzeichnungen*, vol.4, pp.491-2, Bärenreiter 1963.

6) First published in Plath, W.: 'Über Skizzen zu Mozarts Requiem', *Bericht über den Internationalen Musikwissenschaftlichen Kongress, Kassel 1962*, pp.184-7, Kassel 1963.

7) The two volumes are now published in facsimile (see above, note 4).

8) Wolff, C.: 'The Composition and Completion of Mozart's Requiem, 1791-2', in Eisen, C.(ed.): *Mozart Studies*, Clarendon Press, Oxford, 1991.

9) Bach, C.P.E.: *Versuch über die wahre Art das Clavier zu spielen* (two parts, Berlin, 1753 and 1762, reprinted in 1780, 1787 and 1797), translated Mitchell, William J.: *Essay on the true art of playing keyboard instruments*, New York and London, 1949. Eulenberg Edition, p.411, London 1974.

10) Moseley, P.: 'Mozart's Requiem: A re-evaluation of the evidence', *Journal of the Royal Musical Association*, 114 (1989).

11) Bach, C.P.E., Ibid., pp.386-7.

12) Introduction to *Mozart: Requiem*, ed. Beyer, Franz; Zurich, Eulenberg, 1971, 1980.

13) Blume, F.: 'Requiem but no Peace', *The Musical Quarterly*, 17 (1961), pp.147-69.

14) Handke, R.: 'Zur Lösung der Benedictusfrage', *Mozarts Requiem in Zeitschrift für Musikwissenschaft*, 1 (1918), pp.108-30.

15) Marguerre, K.: 'Mozart und Süssmayr', *Mozart-Jahrbuch*, 1962-3, pp.172-7.

16) Maunder, R.: *Mozart's Requiem: on preparing a new edition*, Clarendon Press, Oxford, 1988. See especially pp.33-73.

17) This resemblance was first noticed by R. Lach in 'W.A. Mozart als Theoretiker', *Denkschriften der Akademie der Wissenschaften in Wien (philosophisch-historische Klasse)*, 61 (1918) 1 Abhandlung. The extract from K453b is also given by Maunder (Ibid., p.48).

18) For instance those by Beyer (see above, note 12); Richard Maunder (Oxford University Press, 1988); H.C. Robbins Landon (1989); and Robert Levin (1991).

19) Charlton, David (ed.): *E.T.A. Hoffmann's Musical Writings*, pp.374-5, Cambridge University Press, 1989.

PREFACE

L'histoire de la composition du Requiem de Mozart a un côté étrange, voire fabuleux que l'on retrouve à tous les événements de sa vie. Que nous considérions ses exploits extraordinaires en tant que jeune virtuose et maestro ou l'ampleur de ses mésaventures financières à Vienne à la fin des années 1780, les grands événements de sa vie sont des moins banals. Ce n'est donc nullement surprenant de s'apercevoir que l'on a souvent coloré et brodé la réalité, pour faire ressortir l'élément émotionnel et créer un mythe autour de ce musicien des plus remarquable. L'histoire simple de la création du Requiem est en elle-même frappante: que Mozart, dans les dernières années de sa vie, ait travaillé sur une Messe pour les Morts, que son oeuvre ait été le résultat d'une commission anonyme et que l'envoyé du commissionnaire, pour éviter de donner une adresse, ait dû rendre plusieurs visites à l'improviste, comme un messager d'un autre monde, tout cela peut être facilement gonflé de présages surnaturels.

Même le compte-rendu de Franz Niemetschek[1] publié pour la première fois en 1798, fondé sur les informations données par Constance, la veuve de Mozart, et qui reçut plus tard l'accord "officiel" en étant incorporé à la biographie de Mozart par le second mari de Constance, Georg von Nissen, même Niemetschek parle de l'agent du commissionnaire apparaissant "comme un fantôme", et le compte-rendu de Friedrich Rochlitz[2] va beaucoup plus loin en suggérant que le compositeur était possédé d'un désir démoniaque et fébrile de terminer le Requiem et qu'il sentait la fin s'approcher.

LA COMMISSION DU REQUIEM

Le Requiem de Mozart fut commissionné par le Comte Franz Walsegg-Stuppach (1763-1827) comme messe souvenir pour sa femme qui était morte en février 1791. Le Comte, violoncelliste et flûtiste amateur enthousiaste, avait quelque ambition d'être lui aussi reconnu comme compositeur, et avait en fait composé "quelques vétilles", selon Anton Herzog, son ancien employé et partenaire de quatuor. Le récit d'Herzog[3], rédigé en 1839, ne fut publié qu'en 1964. Il y décrit comment le Comte, lors de soirées de musique de chambre organisées chez lui, encourageait les personnes présentes à deviner que les quatuors interprétés provenaient de partitions manuscrites de son cru. Certaines pages de titre qu'il avait eues en sa possession avaient même le nom de Walsegg substitué à celui du véritable compositeur, Hoffmeister ou Devienne. C'est par la même supercherie qu'il essaya de s'approprier le Requiem de Mozart. Même après sa publication il raconta à Herzog — qui ne le crut pas — qu'il avait été l'élève de Mozart, qu'il lui avait envoyé des parties complètes de "son" Requiem pour obtenir son approbation mais qu'on ne les lui avait rendues qu'après la mort de Mozart et qu'alors commença la legende selon laquelle Mozart en était le compositeur. Le messager "fantôme" serait le Dr Johann Nepomuk Sortschan, un avocat viennois représentant Walsegg dans les affaires.

L'ACHEVEMENT DE L'OEUVRE PAR SÜSSMAYR

Plus important encore que l'origine étrange du Requiem est le fait que Mozart n'ait pu le finir de son vivant, et que l'on ne saura jamais exactement quelle proportion de la version reconnue achevée par Franz Süssmayr (1766-1803) est de Mozart. Dans une lettre datée du 8 septembre 1800 adressée aux éditeurs de Leipzig, Breitkopf et Härtel[4], Süssmayr prétend:

i) que plusieurs compositeurs auraient été contactés pour terminer l'oeuvre avant qu'il n'accepte cette tâche.

ii) qu'il aurait joué et chanté les parties complètes dans leur totalité avec Mozart et très souvent (*sehr oft*) discuté de l'arrangement et de l'orchestration de l'oeuvre avec lui.

iii) que la fin du Lacrimosa et du Sanctus, Benedictus et Agnus Dei seraient de lui (de Süssmayr): "Ganz neu von mir verfertiget".

Süssmayr nous donne aussi une image généralement correcte des parties de la partition écrites par Mozart encore intactes.

Ce qui est surprenant est que si Süssmayr avait bel et bien discuté en detail de l'achèvement du Requiem avec Mozart, pourquoi donc n'avait-il pas été la première personne à être choisie (voir **La Partition d'Origine**, ci-dessous)? Il serait aussi très intéressant, bien sûr, de connaître précisément la nature de toute discussion entre Mozart et Süssmayr (Süssmayr exagérait-il à ce moment-là?) et d'apprendre si les "apports nouveaux" de Süssmayr à la partition étaient fondés sur quelque information écrite ou orale provenant de Mozart. Constance, écrivant plusieurs années plus tard[5], disait être convaincue que Süssmayr avait eu accès à des fragments ("Trümmer") qui étaient l'ébauche des mouvements manquants. Elle se souciait alors de défendre l'authenticité du Requiem face à ceux qui tentaient de le dénoncer comme faux, mais elle avait grand peine à démontrer qu'elle connaissait les méthodes de travail de Mozart et que des ébauches aient pu être écrites.

L'un de ces "Trümmer" est apparu récemment[6]. Au recto de cette unique feuille de papier est une ébauche pour *Die Zauberflöte* et au verso se trouvent deux ébauches rapides pour le Requiem: quatre mesures du Rex Tremendae, et une exposition en fugue sur le mot "Amen", qui devait suivre le Lacrimosa à la fin de la Séquence. Celle-ci ne fut pas utilisée par Süssmayr mais il est clairement possible qu'il ait utilisé des ébauches similaires comme base de ses "nouveaux" mouvements pour le Sanctus, l'Osanna, le Benedictus et l'Agnus Dei.

Nous apprenons aussi de Constance (dans sa lettre à Breitkopf du 27 mars 1799) que l'idée ou la répétition du Kyrie pour former le dernier mouvement n'était pas de Süssmayr mais lui avait été suggérée par Mozart peu avant sa mort.

LA PARTITION D'ORIGINE

Elle tient en deux volumes, tous deux actuellement en la possession de la Musiksammlung de la Nationalbibliotek autrichienne (Mus. Hs. 17.561 a et b)[7]. Le premier est la partition complète que Constance présenta au Comte Walsegg, comprenant le manuscrit d'origine de Mozart pour l'Introit et le Kyrie, le premier entièrement de sa composition, le dernier augmenté des parties pour trompette et timbales de la main de Süssmayr, et les parties d'accompagnement pour violons, alto, cors de basset et bassons écrites par un autre élève de Mozart, Franz Jacob Freystädler (1761-1844). Freystädler fit quelques fautes de base en transposant les parties des cors de basset. Le reste de cette partition est entièrement de Süssmayr, sans aucune distinction entre ses contributions et celles de Mozart. Le second volume comprend la version originale incomplète de Mozart pour les mouvements qui forment la Séquence (Dies Irae, Tuba Mirum, Rex Tremendae, Recordare, Confutatis et Lacrimosa) et l'Offertorium (Domine Jesu et Hostias). Pour tous ces mouvements, sauf le Lacrimosa dont il n'a écrit que les 8 premières mesures, Mozart a produit une première version complète des choeurs et des basses instrumentales. Il a numéroté, soigneusement ceci dans l'Introit, le Kyrie, le Dies Irae, le Confutatis et dans une partie du Domine Jesu. Il a aussi fourni les quelques conseils suivants pour l'instrumentation:

Dies Irae
Mesures 1 à 4: 1ers et 2èmes violons, alto; 5 à 10: 1er violon; 19 à 31 (premier temps): 1er violon; 40 (milieu) à 57: 1er violon; 65-8: 1er violon.

Tuba Mirum
Mesures 1 à 18: trombone solo; 44: 1ers et 2èmes violons; 45 à 62: 1er violon.

Rex Tremendae
Mesures 1 à 20: 1er violon; 22: 1er violon.

Recordare
Mesures 1 à 7: cors de basset; 1 à 14 (premier temps): 1ers et 2èmes violons, alto (Mozart indique des pauses aux mesures 1-6): 34-8 (1ère note): 1er violon; 52-3: 1er violon, alto; 63 à 79: 1er violon; 109-10: 1ers et 2èmes violons; 126 à 130: 1ers violons; 126-8: 2ème violon, alto.

Confutatis
Mesures 7 à 12: 1er violon; 17 à 40: 1er violon; 26-9: cors de basset, bassons; 38 (dernier temps) à 40: 2ème violon.

Lacrimosa
Mesures 1-2: 1ers et 2èmes violons, alto.

Domine Jesu
Mesures 43 (troisième temps) à 46 (premier temps): 1er violon; 67 à 71 (premier temps): 1ers et 2èmes violons; 71-8: 1er violon.

Hostias
Mesures 1-2: 1ers et 2èmes violons, alto; 44-5 1ers et 2èmes violons; 46 à 54: 1er violon.

Dans les mouvements de la Séquence cette partition comprend aussi les tentatives faites par Joseph Eybler pour achever le Requiem. Plus tard, on essaya, sans toujours tomber juste, de distinguer l'écriture de Mozart de celle d'Eybler en mettant les additions d'Eybler entre parenthèses au crayon de papier, les parties d'origine étant étiquetées "Moz" ou "Mozart". On notera la tentative particulièrement intéressante d'Eybler de continuer le Lacrimosa pendant 2 mesures.*

CETTE EDITION

La Nouvelle Edition Chorale de Novello présente deux versions du Requiem de Mozart. L'ancienne édition de la version traditionnelle (achevée par Süssmayr) a été révisée afin qu'elle corresponde exactement à la partition d'origine de Mozart/Süssmayr. Bien qu'en général Süssmayr ait recopié le manuscrit de Mozart de façon rigoureuse, il n'a pu éviter quelques erreurs, et l'on trouve même occasionnellement des exemples où la version originale de Mozart a été délibérément modifiée. Notre édition restaure l'original. La nouvelle partition chorale est ainsi faite qu'on peut l'utiliser avec l'ancienne édition de Novello, avec la même mise en page et pagination, cependant, la réduction d'orchestre a été modifiée afin qu'elle donne une image plus juste de l'arrangement de l'orchestre.

Cette édition propose en plus de la version achevée par Süssmayr ma propre version comme alternative. Pour les mouvements où Mozart avait composé les parties chorales, la version alternative apparaît dans la partition des choeurs en guise de réduction d'orchestre différente, quand ma version est suffisamment éloignée de celle de Süssmayr pour qu'elle le réclame. Les mouvements où la partie chorale de Mozart est incomplète ou inexistante (Lacrimosa, Benedictus et Agnus Dei) sont cependant représentés intégralement. Quelques problèmes d'édition spécifiques méritent une courte explication que voici:

LES TROMBONES

A la mesure 7 de l'Introit, la mesure précédant la première entrée des choeurs, Mozart note une

*Il semble probable que Maximilian Stadler ait lui aussi joué un rôle dans l'achèvement du Requiem. Dans un article récent, Christoph Wolff[8] discute du fait qu'il est évident que Maximilian a préparé des parties instrumentales pour le Domine Jesu et l'Hostias.

entrée des trombones sur les portées des trois choeurs les plus bas; on suppose qu'ils continuent à jouer *colla parte* avec l'alto, le ténor et la basse. Süssmayr ne mentionne les trombones spécifiquement que dans le Dies Irae, le Tuba Mirum (un prolongement du solo de Mozart pour le trombone ténor du début du mouvement), le Rex Tremendae, le Confutatis, le Lacrimosa, le Domine Deus, le Benedictus et l'Agnus Dei. Quand les parties instrumentales du Requiem furent publiées pour la première fois (à Vienne, en 1812), les parties *colla voce* pour 3 trombones étaient aussi fournies pour l'Introit, le Kyrie, le Sanctus et le Communio (Lux Aeterna). En général j'ai suivi l'exemple de cette édition, ajoutant seulement des parties *colla voce* pour la fin du premier Osanna, ce qui n'est pas inclus dans l'édition de 1812.

LA DYNAMIQUE

Dans l'Hostias, la première indication dynamique que l'on trouve dans le manuscrit de Mozart est le *piano* sur le 3ème temps de la mesure 24 (Süssmayr indique *forte* pour les parties des vents à la mesure 23, mais rien plus tôt). Au 18ème siècle on jouait *forte* à moins que les indications ne soient contraires. Cela signifie-t-il que l'ouverture du mouvement doive être *forte?* J'imagine que beaucoup d'interprètes de nos jours n'aimeraient guère commencer ce mouvement en jouant fort. Même Süssmayr, en écrivant *senza tromboni* au début suggère une approche plus délicate. Il me semble que dans une telle situation c'est au chef d'orchestre de trancher pour ce qui lui paraît l'approche la plus convaincante.*

"SOLO" ET "TUTTI"

Dans le Benedictus, Süssmayr note les 2 premières entrées chorales (alto et soprano) "solo", mais quand le ténor et la basse entrent en scène comme à la mesure 10, il n'y a aucune indication de "solo" ni de "tutti". Il n'indique rien non plus plus tard dans le mouvement — même pas pour l'Osanna. Il semble possible qu'il ait voulu que ce soient les choeurs aux mesures 10 à 27 et à partir de la mesure 33. De plus, cette solution expliquerait une partition surchargée, trombones inclus, que l'on peut particulièrement remarquer aux mesures 10 à 18.

LE TEMPO

Mozart a fourni des indications de tempo uniquement pour l'Introit, le Kyrie, le Tuba Mirum et le Confutatis. Pour le Rex Tremendae, on a suggéré *Adagio*, par analogie avec le Gratias Agimus de la Messe en Do Mineur. Pour le Recordare, je suggérerais *Andante*. L'équivalent le plus proche que j'aie trouvé est le "Tamino mein! O welch'ein Gluck" de Pamina dans la finale du 2nd acte de *Die Zauberflöte*. On suggère *Larghetto*

*C'est grâce à Robert Levin que ce problème a été souligné.

pour le Lacrimosa (de même que pour l'Agnus Dei, pour lequel Süssmayr ne fournit aucune indication de tempo). Süssmayr propose *Andante con moto* pour le Domine Deus; un *Allegro* ou *Allegro moderato* serait peut-être plus heureux (faites la comparaison avec le Confiteor des Vesprae Solennes de Confessore, K.339). L'*Andante* de Süssmayr pour l'Hostias est moins discutable. J'ai aussi fourni de nouvelles suggestions de tempo métronome. Celles-ci devraient être considérées comme approximatives — en prenant en compte l'acoustique, la taille de la chorale et autres considérations. Là où il existait des mouvements comparables qui comportaient des indications de tempo métronome (on a commencé à utiliser le métronome dans les années 1810), je m'en suis inspiré, pour les mouvements *Adagio* en 4/4 par exemple.

LES LIAISONS

Dans la partition d'origine, Mozart, suivant sa pratique habituelle en musique chorale, indique les divisions syllabiques au moyen de liaisons ou de groupes de croches et demi-croches. Dans cette édition ces liaisons n'apparaissent pas, mais on doit se rappeler que, pour Mozart, la liaison fonctionne en tant qu' indication de phrasé mais aussi pour montrer l'ensemble des notes chantées pour une syllabe. Ainsi les notes couplées dans la phrase "Quantus tremor est futurus" (Dies Irae, à partir de la mesure 41) doivent être appuyées, mais les melismas plus longs comme ceux du Domine Jesu (mesures 35 à 40) indiquent une ligne uniforme et soutenue. Par contre Mozart ne lie pas les longs melismas du Kyrie, ce qui indique une prononciation plus articulée. Les quelques liaisons dans les parties chorales sont confinées aux endroits où le modèle de liaison de Mozart ne suit pas exactement la division syllabique. Dans les parties "de Süssmayr" (à partir du Sanctus) il n'y a pas de liaisons chorales. Dans sa première version, Süssmayr est moins cohérent dans sa façon d'ajouter des liaisons et quand celles-ci ne correspondent pas à la division syllabique, il est difficile de croire qu'on a voulu obtenir un phrasé spécifique.

LA BASSE CONTINUE

Il est clair que Mozart a voulu donner une basse méticuleusement chiffrée pour le Requiem, suivant le précepte de C.P.E. Bach d'après lequel "rien de ce qui est nécessaire et essentiel ne saurait être pris à la légère"[9]. Il a chiffré les 3 premières parties (l'Introit, le Kyrie† et le Dies Irae), la 2ème mesure du Rex Tremendae, le Confutatis (à partir de la mesure 26) et les mesures 21-8 du Domine Jesu. Ces chiffres peuvent nous donner d'inestimables indices pour l'achèvement de l'orchestration, par exemple les accords de

†Paul Moseley[10] a récemment fait remarquer qu'à partir de la mesure 20 du Kyrie (mesure 68 dans notre édition) le chiffrage est de Süssmayr.

9ème du Domine Jesu, ignorés par Süssmayr. En écrivant "organo e basso" au debut sur la portée la plus basse de la partition, Mozart a spécifié la participation supplémentaire d'un orgue dans le Recordare, le Lacrimosa et l'Hostias. Aucun orgue n'est mentionné pour le Tuba Mirum. On peut se demander si ce n'est pas une omission; peut-être Mozart voulait-il que l'orgue joue pendant tout le Requiem, sauf aux endroits où "senza organo" est spécifiquement indiqué? Il demande bien un orgue pour le Recordare, qui est un autre mouvement solo avec une basse non chiffrée. Il est cependant possible que des interprètes de nos jours aient l'impression que la basse continue n'apporte guère à aucun de ces deux mouvements et préfèrent l'omettre. Etant donné que le Recordare est le seul mouvement où Mozart demande un orgue et qu'après il ne donne aucune autre indication, se pourrait-il que cet "organo e basso" soit une erreur?

Süssmayr a non seulement recopié les chiffres de Mozart mais aussi ajouté une basse chiffrée pour terminer le Lacrimosa, terminé le chiffrage de Mozart pour le Domine Jesu (sauf pour les 7 dernières mesures) et fourni des chiffres pour ses versions du Sanctus, de l'Agnus Dei, et, de façon plus sporadique, du Benedictus. Pour ma version, suivant l'exemple probable de Mozart au Tuba Mirum, je n'ai pas voulu d'orgue pour le Benedictus, mais ai ajouté ailleurs une basse chiffrée (il n'y a pas de chiffrage dans la partition des choeurs, mais dans la partition d'ensemble qui est disponible pour la location à Novello). J'ai aussi fourni une partie pour la basse continue (aussi pour la location), produisant une basse chiffrée couvrant toute l'oeuvre. En suivant l'exemple de plusieurs éditions modernes (la New Mozart Edition de Bärenreiter, par exemple), j'ai couplé les chiffres de Mozart et Süssmayr en utilisant le chiffrage que l'on trouve dans la 1ère édition des parties instrumentales du Requiem (Vienne, 1812).

J'ai gardé ma partie de basse continue aussi simple que possible, suivant encore une fois la règle de C.P.E. Bach qu'un tel accompagnement devrait avant tout être discret.[11] Le *Versuch über die wahre Art das Clavier zu spielen* de Bach fournit, dans sa rubrique sur l'accompagnement, le meilleur guide de l'époque pour toute personne souhaitant le réaliser par eux-mêmes. Ma version pour l'orgue ne devrait de toute façon être regardée que comme un guide: en prenant en considération l'instrument et la marque utilisés, le nombre de musiciens et l'acoustique de l'église ou de la salle de concert, des notes pouvant être ajoutées ou enlevées pour un meilleur équilibre.

REFLEXION AU SUJET DE LA NOUVELLE VERSION

Le travail de Süssmayr sur le Requiem de Mozart est double: l'achèvement de la mise en musique instrumentale là où Mozart avait fourni une première version complète des parties chorales et de la ligne de basse, et le travail de composition qu'il a dû faire en écrivant ou achevant les autres parties. Bien que l'oeuvre dans son ensemble s'est révélée être l'une des plus aimées et admirées de Mozart, il a toujours été clair depuis sa première parution qu'il manque quelquefois la perfection de détail, le travail d'un homme connaissant bien son métier, le rapport imaginatif entre la matière de second plan avec le tout, qui sont si caractéristiques des autres derniers chefs-d'oeuvres de Mozart. L'orchestration de Süssmayr, la plupart du temps parfaitement professionelle, quelquefois inepte, mais rarement imaginative, n'endommage pas souvent la version de Mozart mais la flatte rarement. En ce qui concerne les parties dont Süssmayr se prétend l'auteur elles contiennent des défauts plus graves: la superficialité des fugues de l'Osanna, la stagnation harmonique dans la partie centrale du Benedictus sont deux tels exemples décevants. Pourtant les idées principales de toutes les parties, qu'elles proviennent de Mozart ou qu'elles aient été composées par Süssmayr seul semblent bien maintenir l'unité et le caractère de l'oeuvre. La question de savoir quelles parties des mouvements, si tant est qu'il les ait composées, sont de Mozart, a été souvent débattue, et Beyer[12], Blume[13], Handke[14], Marguerre[15], Maunder[16], Moseley, Wolff, et bien d'autres, ont des conclusions bien différentes. Je ne tenterais pas d'ouvrir le débat ici, sauf si ce n'est pour observer combien il est difficile de prouver ou d'infirmer l'identité du compositeur sur des bases stylistiques. La version de Süssmayr, de toute façon, bénéficiera toujours d'un statut particulier, parce que c'est celle qui a longtemps été interprétée et la seule d'un compositeur viennois des années 1790 qui, de plus, fut le mieux placé pour connaître les intentions de Mozart.

Toute personne se trouvant devant la tâche d'achever le Requiem aujourd'hui, est confrontée à des problèmes sérieux. Il n'est pas possible de ne se reposer que sur des parallèles avec d'autres oeuvres de Mozart; l'orchestration hors du commun du Requiem, et l'absence de toute grande oeuvre sacrée comparable dans ses dernières années en est la raison. Si nous accordons de l'importance jusqu'à la vie et l'individualité intenses des détails secondaires dans la musique de Mozart, nous lui rendrions en tous cas un très mauvais service en ne faisant que répéter des motifs pris de ses autres oeuvres. Tout en restant perceptif aux moindres possibilités de parallèles vraiment conséquents dans d'autres oeuvres de Mozart, j'ai essayé, d'une façon générale, de me mettre dans la position d'un compositeur viennois de l'époque de Mozart, tentant d'achever la grande structure de l'oeuvre de la manière la plus convaincante. Pour le Lacrimosa j'ai commencé par imiter la tentative de Joseph Eybler pour le continuer et j'ai construit un mouvement dont la structure rappelle celle du Dies Irae au début de la Séquence. Le Sanctus est une adaption de la version de Süssmayr. Pour le Benedictus j'ai utilisé les idées principales de la version traditionnelle (la phrase d'ouverture est de Mozart de toute façon – on la trouve dans K453b, le cahier d'exercices pour Barbara Ployer[17]) et ai composé un nouveau mouvement, utilisant une série de modèles et d'indices mozartiens. De l'Agnus Dei, communément reconnu comme le mouvement le plus convaincant "de Süssmayr", j'ai gardé les parties chorales et de basse, jusqu'à sa partie finale, mais j'ai ajouté une introduction instrumentale plus longue pour le Lux Aeterna*; il me semblait important de réintroduire l'atmosphère et les idées de l'Introit de façon plus décisive. Pour les fugues des choeurs sur "Amen" et "Osanna", j'ai surtout utilisé comme modèles les morceaux de fugue du Requiem terminé par Mozart – le Kyrie et le Quam Olim Abrahae – le Cum Sancto Spiritu de la Messe en Do Mineur K427 et les fugues instrumentales comme celle en Do Mineur K426. Le point de départ pour l'Amen était l'ébauche courte dont on a déjà parlé; pour l'Osanna j'ai utilisé le sujet de la version de

*Ceci a posé un problème pour numéroter les mesures. Dans la version de Süssmayr, l'Agnus Dei et le Communio ont été numérotés ensemble; pour la nouvelle l'Agnus Dei et les six premières mesures du Lux Aeterna ont été numérotés séparément, rejoignant la numérotation de Süssmayr à la mesure 53.

Süssmayr. Avec l'Amen et cette version plus allongée de l'Osanna en plus des autres mouvements chorals de grande envergure, la prépondérance chorale de l'oeuvre entière, avec ses caractéristiques impressionnantes, délibérément archaïques dans leur contrepoint, devient même plus claire.

Plusieurs autres versions du Requiem de Mozart ont été produites ces dernières années[18], chacune ayant son propre point de vue sur les "améliorations" plus que nécessaires. Cette multiplicité de productions reflète clairement le niveau d'intérêt actuel élevé pour la musique de Mozart, et me paraît être un bon signe. Le Requiem est avant tout l'oeuvre majeure de Mozart pour laquelle aucune version définitive n'existe. On peut apprendre beaucoup et être plus qu'inspiré par elle, si on la considère de différents points de vue. Quelques aspects de la vision de Mozart auront été obscurcis par l'intervention de l'un ou au contraire rehaussés par un autre. En 1814, E.T.A. Hoffmann s'était déjà rendu compte des qualités du Requiem quand il écrivit que "la musique reste dévotionnelle du début jusqu'à la fin; une pure dévotion résonne à travers ces accords qui parlent d'un autre monde en inspirant le respect et l'admiration, et qui sont eux-même un autre monde dans leur pouvoir et dignité singuliers."[19]

DUNCAN DRUCE, Holmbridge, juin 1992

Notes

1) Niemetschek, Franz Xaver. *Leben des k.k. Kapellmeisters Wolfgang Gottlieb Mozart* (Prague 1798).
2) Rochlitz, Friedrich. 'Verbürgte Anekdoten aus Wolfgang Gottlieb Mozarts Leben', *Allgemeine Musikalische Zeitung*, Leipzig, Oct-Dec. 1798.
3) Herzog, Anton: *Wahre und ausführliche Geschichte des Requiem von W.A. Mozart*.
4) Publiée dans l'introduction à l'édition facsimile de Bärenreiter de la partition d'origine du Requiem, Kassel, 1990.
5) Lettre adressée à Maximilian Stadler du 14.3.1827. Bauer, A. et Deutsch, O.E.(ed.): *Mozart: Briefe und Aufzeichnungen*, vol.4, pp.491-2, Bärenreiter 1963.
6) Publié pour la première fois dans Plath, W.: 'Über Skizzen zu Mozarts Requiem', *Bericht über den Internationalen Musikwissenschaftlichen Kongress, Kassel 1962*, pp.184-7, Kassel 1963.
7) Les deux volumes sont maintenant publiés en facsimile (voir ci-dessus, note 4).
8) Wolff, C.: 'The Composition and Completion of Mozart's Requiem, 1791-2', *Mozart Studies*, ed. Eisen, C., Clarendon Press, Oxford, 1991.
9) Bach, C.P.E.: *Versuch über die wahre Art das Clavier zu spielen* (deux parties, Berlin, 1753 et 1762, réimprimées en 1780, 1787 et 1797).

10) Moseley, P.: 'Mozart's Requiem: A re-evaluation of the evidence', *Journal of the Royal Musical Association*, 114 (1989).
11) Bach, C.P.E., Ibid., pp.386-7.
12) Introduction à *Mozart: Requiem*, ed. Beyer, Franz; Zurich, Eulenberg, 1971, 1980.
13) Blume, F.: 'Requiem but no Peace', *The Musical Quarterly*, 17 (1961), pp.147-69.
14) Handke, R.: 'Zur Lösung der Benedictusfrage', *Mozarts Requiem in Zeitschrift für Musikwissenschaft*, 1 (1918), pp. 108-30.
15) Marguerre, K.: 'Mozart und Süssmayr', *Mozart-Jahrbuch*, 1962-3, pp.172-7.
16) Maunder, R.: *Mozart's Requiem: on preparing a new edition*, Clarendon Press, Oxford, 1988. Voir spécialement pp.33 à 73.
17) Cette ressemblance fut remarquée pour la première fois par R. Lach dans 'W.A. Mozart als Theoretiker', *Denkschriften der Akademie der Wissenschaften in Wien (philosophisch-historische Klasse)*, 61 (1918) 1 Abhandlung. L'extrait de K453b est aussi donné par Maunder (Ibid., p.48).
18) Par exemple ceux de Beyer (voir ci-dessus, note 12); Richard Maunder (Oxford University Press, 1988); H.C. Robbins Landon (1989); et Robert Levin (1991).
19) Charlton, David (ed.): *E.T.A. Hoffmann's Musical Writings*, pp.374-5, Cambridge University Press, 1989.

VORWORT

Die Kompositionsgeschichte von Mozarts Requiem hat eine merkwürdige, sagenhafte Qualität, die sehr typisch für die Ereignisse in Mozarts Leben ist. Ob man seine erstaunlichen Leistungen und Werke als junger Virtuose und Maestro oder die Tiefe seines finanziellen Unglücks in Wien in den späten 1780er Jahren betrachtet, kaum eines seiner biographischen Daten ist ohne einen interessanten Bezug. Es überrascht daher nicht, wenn man feststellt, daß diese Tatsachen oft geschönt und ausgeschmückt wurden, um ihren emotionalen Effekt zu verstärken und eine Legende um diesen bemerkenswerten Musiker zu ranken. Die einfache Geschichte der Entstehung des Requiems ist allein schon bemerkenswert – in seinen letzten Lebenswochen arbeitete Mozart an einer Totenmesse, die das Ergebnis eines anonymen Auftrags war; der Bote des Auftraggebers stattete Mozart zahlreiche unangekündigte Besuche ab, – wie ein Besucher aus einer anderen Welt, um keine Adresse hinterlassen zu müssen. Diese Geschichte läßt sich leicht mit Anspielungen auf das Übernatürliche ausschmücken.

Selbst der Bericht von Franz Niemetschek[1], der erstmals 1798 veröffentlicht wurde und auf Informationen von Mozarts Witwe Constanze beruhte, spricht von dem Boten des Auftraggebers, der "wie ein Geist" erschien. Er wurde später offiziell für gut befunden und in die Mozartbiographie von Constanzes zweitem Mann, Georg von Nissen, aufgenommen. Die Schilderung von Friedrich Rochlitz[2] geht sogar noch weiter und stellt Vermutungen an, wonach der Komponist von dem dämonischen und fieberhaften Verlangen, das Requiem fertigzustellen, besessen gewesen sei und sich des nahenden Unheils bewußt gewesen wäre.

DIE BESTELLUNG DES REQUIEMS

Mozarts Requiem war von Graf Franz Walsegg-Stuppach (1763-1827) zum Gedenken an seine Frau in Auftrag gegeben worden, die im Februar 1791 gestorben war. Der Graf, ein eifriger Amateur-Cellist und Flötist, wollte auch als Komponist bekannt sein, und hatte laut Anton Herzog, einem früheren Angestellten und Quartettpartner, "einige Kleinigkeiten" komponiert. Herzogs Bericht[3], 1839 niedergeschrieben, wurde erst 1964 veröffentlicht. Er beschreibt in ihm, wie der Graf an Kammermusikabenden in seinem Haus, die Anwesenden zu den Vermutungen ermuntern würde, daß er die Quartette, die aus Handschriften gespielt wurden, selbst komponiert hatte. Auf den Titelseiten von Partituren aus seinem früheren Besitz wurde sogar der Name des rechtmäßigen Komponisten, Hoffmeister oder Devienne, durch den Namen Walsegg ersetzt. Er bemühte sich, dieselbe Täuschung auch bezüglich Mozarts Requiem aufrechtzuerhalten. Sogar nach seiner Veröffentlichung erzählte er Herzog (der ihm nicht glaubte), daß er Mozarts Schüler gewesen sei, vollständige Teile "seines" Requiems an Mozart zur Ansicht geschickt habe, sie aber erst nach Mozarts Tod zurückbekommen habe. Der Legende nach habe daher Mozart dasselbe komponiert. Der "Geisterbote" war Dr Johann Nepomuk Sortschan, ein Wiener Rechtsanwalt und Walseggs Geschäftsvertreter.

SÜSSMAYRS ERGÄNZUNG

Wichtiger als die Vermutungen über die Ursprünge des Requiems ist die bekannte Tatsache, daß Mozart dessen Vollendung nicht mehr erlebte, und das wahrscheinlich unlösbare Problem, festzustellen, wieviel von der bekannten Fassung, die Franz Süßmayr (1766-1803) ergänzte, wirklich von Mozart stammt. Süßmayr behauptet in einem Brief vom 8. September 1800 an den Leipziger Verleger Breitkopf & Härtel[4]:

i) Daß verschiedene Komponisten darum gebeten worden waren, das Werk fertigzustellen, bevor er diese Aufgabe übernahm

ii) Daß er die fertiggestellten Teile mit Mozart durchgespielt und gesungen habe und "sehr oft" über die Ausarbeitung und Instrumentierung des Werks mit ihm gesprochen habe.

iii) Daß die Ergänzungen von Lacrimosa und Sanctus, Benedictus und Agnus Dei von ihm [Süßmayr] "ganz neu... verfertigt" worden seien.

Von Süßmayr erhalten wir auch ein ziemlich genaues Bild, welche Teile der Partitur in Mozarts Handschrift erhalten sind.

Überraschend ist folgendes: wenn Süßmayr tatsächlich die Fertigstellung des Requiems mit Mozart detailliert besprochen hatte, warum fiel die Wahl nicht gleich auf ihn (vergleiche unten **Die Handschriften**)? Es wäre natürlich auch von großem Interesse, Genaueres über die Gespräche zwischen Mozart und Süßmayr zu erfahren (übertrieb Süßmayr in dieser Hinsicht?) und zu hören, ob die neuen Partiturteile von Süßmayr auf schriftlichen oder mündlichen Aussagen Mozarts beruhen. Constanze schrieb einige Jahre später[5], sie glaube, daß Süßmayr Zugang zu Fragmenten ("Trümmer") hatte, die das Material der "fehlenden" Sätze dokumentierten. Zu jenem Zeitpunkt war sie bemüht, die Echtheit des Requiems vor jenen zu verteidigen, die es als Fälschung bloßstellen wollten. Sie betonte nachdrücklich, daß sie Mozarts Arbeitsmethoden kenne und es wahrscheinlich sei, daß er Skizzen geschrieben habe.

Ein solcher "Trümm" ist kürzlich aufgetaucht[6]. Das Einzelblatt enthält auf der einen Seite eine Skizze für *Die Zauberflöte* und auf der anderen zwei kurze Entwürfe für das Requiem: vier Takte des Rex Tremendae, und eine Themenaufstellung zum "Amen", die dem Lacrimosa am Ende der Sequenz folgen sollte. Letztere wurde von Süßmayr nicht verwendet; es ist jedoch durchaus möglich, daß er ähnliche Skizzen für Sanctus, Osanna, Benedictus und Agnus Dei als Grundlage für seine "neuen" Sätze verwendete.

Von Constanze erfahren wir auch (in ihrem Brief an Breitkopf vom 27. März 1799), daß die Idee der Wiederholung des Kyrie als letzter Satz nicht von Süßmayr stammte, sondern ein Vorschlag Mozarts kurz vor seinem Tod war.

DIE HANDSCHRIFTEN

Die Originalhandschriften des Requiems sind in zwei Bänden enthalten, die sich in der Musiksammlung der Österreichischen Nationalbibliothek (Mus. Hs. 17.561 a und b)[7] befinden. Bei der ersten handelt es sich um die vollständige Partitur, die Constanze Graf Walsegg gab und Mozarts Autograph des Introitus und Kyrie enthält. Das Introitus war von ihm ergänzt worden, das Kyrie mit Trompeten und Paukenteilen steht in Süßmayrs Handschrift. Die Verdoppelungsteile für Violinen, Viola, Bassetthörner und Posaunen waren von Franz Jacob Freystädtler (1761-1841), einem anderen Schüler Mozarts, geschrieben worden. Freystädtler machte viele grundlegende Fehler, als er die Transpositionsteile für Bassetthörner schrieb. Der Rest der Partitur steht in Süßmayrs Handschrift ohne Unterscheidung zwischen seinen und Mozarts Beiträgen. Der zweite Band enthält die unvollständige Partiturskizze der Sätze in Mozarts Handschrift, die die Sequenz (Dies Irae, Tuba Mirum, Rex Tremendae, Recordare, Confutatis und Lacrimosa) bilden, und das Offertorium (Domine Jesu und Hostias). Mozart lieferte für all diese Teile — mit Ausnahme des Lacrimosa, wo er nur die ersten acht Takte niederschrieb — einen vollständigen Entwurf der Gesangsteile und des bezifferten Basses. Er figurierte diesen im Introitus, Kyrie, Dies Irae, Confutatis und in Teilen des Domine Jesu. Er machte auch einige Angaben bezüglich der Instrumentierung, und zwar:

Dies Irae
Takte 1-4, 1. und 2. Violine, Viola; 5-10, 1. Violine; 19-31 (erster Schlag) 1. Violine; 40 (Mitte)-57, 1. Violine; 65-68, 1. Violine.

Tuba Mirum
Takte 1-18, Soloposaune; 44, 1. und 2. Violine; 45-62, 1. Violine.

Rex Tremendae
Takte 1-20, 1. Violine; 22, 1. Violine.

Recordare
Takte 1-7, Bassetthörner; 1-14 (erster Schlag), 1. und 2. Violine, Viola (Mozart schrieb Pausen in den Takten 1-6); 34-38 (erste Note), 1. Violine; 52-53, 1. Violine, Viola; 68-79, 1. Violine; 109-110, 1. und 2. Violine; 126-130, 1. Violine; 126-128, 2. Violine, Viola.

Confutatis
Takte 7-12, 1. Violine; 17-40, 1. Violine; 26-29, Bassetthörner, Posaunen; 38 (letzter Schlag)-40, 2. Violine.

Lacrimosa
Takte 1-2, 1. und 2. Violine, Viola.

Domine Jesu
Takte 43 (dritter Schlag)-46 (erster Schlag), 1. Violine; 67-71 (erster Schlag), 1. und 2. Violine; 71-78, 1. Violine.

Hostias
Takte 1-2, 1. und 2. Violine, Viola; 44-45, 1. und 2. Violine; 46-54, 1. Violine.

In den Sätzen der Sequenz enthält diese Partitur auch die Versuche von Joseph Eybler, die Systeme zu ergänzen. Eybler (1765-1846), der spätere Wiener Hofkapellmeister, scheint der erste Komponist gewesen zu sein, an den sich Constanze wegen der Fertigstellung des Requiems wandte. Es wurde später versucht — nicht immer einwandfrei — Mozarts Aufzeichnungen von denen Eyblers durch Bleistiftumrandungen abzugrenzen. Die Originalteile wurden 'Moz' oder 'Mozart' überschrieben. Eyblers zweitaktiger Versuch einer Ergänzung des Lacrimosa ist von besonderem Interesse.*

DIESE AUSGABE

Die Neue Novello Ausgabe für Chor enthält zwei Versionen von Mozarts Requiem. Die vorhergehende Ausgabe der traditionellen Version (von Süßmayr ergänzt) wurde so überarbeitet, daß sie völlig mit der Mozart/Süßmayr-Handschrift übereinstimmt. Obwohl Süßmayr Mozarts Manuskript in der Regel exakt kopierte, machte er doch einige Fehler. Es gibt sogar einige wenige Fälle, in denen er absichtlich Mozarts Original änderte. Wir sind hier wieder zu Mozart zurückgekehrt. Die neue Vokalpartitur ist so angelegt, daß sie neben der früheren Novelloausgabe benutzt werden kann; die Anordnung der Seiten und die Numerierung ist dieselbe. Der Klavierauszug wurde jedoch überarbeitet, damit er ein genaueres Bild der Orchesterfassung wiedergibt.

Die vorliegende Ausgabe enthält neben der Süßmayr-Ergänzung meine eigene Bearbeitung des Requiems als Alternative. In jenen Sätzen, für die Mozart die Vokalteile komponierte, erscheint die Alternative in der Gesangspartitur in Verkleidung eines anderen Klavierauszugs, insofern meine Ergänzung der Instrumentierung sich von der Süßmayrs grundlegend unterscheidet. Jene Sätze, für die das Mozartoriginal vokal unvollständig oder gar

*Es erscheint wahrscheinlich, daß Maximilian Stadler ebenfalls an der Fertigstellung des Requiems beteiligt war. Christoph Wolff[8] setzt sich in einem kürzlich veröffentlichten Artikel mit den Beweisen auseinander, daß Stadler Instrumentalstücke für das Domine Jesu und Hostias entwarf.

nicht vorhanden ist (Lacrimosa, Amen, Sanctus, Benedictus und Agnus Dei), werden vollständig wiedergegeben. Einige wenige spezifische Editionsprobleme sollen hier kurz angesprochen werden:

DIE POSAUNEN

Im 7. Takt des Introitus, dem Takt vor dem ersten Choreinsatz, sieht Mozart einen Posauneneinsatz auf den unteren drei Systemen des Vokalteils vor. Er geht davon aus, daß sie weiter *colla parte* spielen, zusammen mit Alt, Tenor und Bass. Süßmayr führt Posaunen nur im Dies Irae, Tuba Mirum (eine Ausweitung von Mozarts Solo für Tenorposaune zu Beginn des Satzes), Rex Tremendae, Confutatis, Lacrimosa, Domine Deus, Benedictus und Agnus Dei an. Als instrumentale Teile des Requiems erstmals veröffentlicht wurden (Wien, 1812), gab es auch *colla voce*-Teile für drei Posaunen im Introitus, Kyrie, Sanctus und Communio (Lux Aeterna). Ich folge im allgemeinen dem Beispiel dieser Ausgabe und habe *colla voce*-Teile, die in der Fassung von 1812 nicht vorhanden waren, nur am Ende des ersten Osanna ergänzt.

DYNAMIK

Im Hostias findet sich die erste dynamische Angabe in Mozarts Partiturskizze im *piano* auf dem dritten Schlag von Takt 24 (Süßmayr schrieb *forte* für die Bläserteile in Takt 23, aber nicht vorher). Im 18. Jahrhundert war *forte* die vorherrschende Dynamik und untersagte andere Angaben. Bedeutet dies, daß der Anfang dieses Satzes *forte* sein sollte? Ich nehme an, daß viele heutige Ausführende diesen Satz nur ungern laut beginnen würden. Selbst Süßmayr schlug einen leiseren Anfang vor, als er *senza tromboni* schrieb. In einer solchen Situation hängt die Entscheidung, wie das Stück am überzeugendsten angegangen werden soll, meiner Meinung nach vom Dirigenten ab.*

'SOLO' UND 'TUTTI'

Im Benedictus markiert Süßmayr die zuerst einsetzenden zwei Stimmen (Alt und Sopran) mit 'solo'. Beim Einsatz von Tenor und Bass in Takt 10 gibt es jedoch keine Kennzeichnungen von 'solo' oder 'tutti'. Auch macht er später im Satz keine Angaben − noch nicht einmal für das Osanna. Es erscheint zumindest möglich, daß die Takte 10-27 und ab Takt 33 vom Chor ausgeführt werden sollten. Diese Lösung wäre auch eine Erklärung für die große Besetzung − einschließlich Posaunen − besonders in den Takten 10-18.

*Ich bin Robert Levin dankbar, daß er mich auf dieses Problem aufmerksam machte.

TEMPO

Mozart machte nur Tempoangaben für die Sätze Introitus, Dies Irae, Tuba Mirum und Confutatis. Man hatte *Adagio* für das Rex Tremendae vorgeschlagen in Analogie zu dem Gratias Agimus der c-moll Messe. Für das Recordare würde ich *Andante* empfehlen. Am nächsten kommt ihm Paminas "Tamino mein! O welch' ein Glück' aus dem Finale vom zweiten Akt der *Zauberflöte*. *Larghetto* wurde für das Lacrimosa vorgeschlagen (sowie für das Agnus Dei, für das Süßmayr keine Tempoangaben machte). Süßmayr schlägt *Andante con moto* für Dominus Deus vor; *Allegro* oder *Allegro moderato* mögen glaubhafter scheinen (man vergleiche das Confitebor aus der Vesprae Solennes de Confessore, KV 339). Süßmayrs *Andante* für das Hostias ist weniger umstritten. Ich habe auch neue Metronomangaben vorgeschlagen. Diese sollten jedoch nur als eine Annäherung aufgefaßt werden −je nach Akustik, Größe des Chors und anderen Erwägungen. In den Fällen, wo frühe Metronomangaben für vergleichbare Sätze vorhanden sind (das Metronom wurde seit der zweiten Hälfte des 19. Jahrhunderts benutzt), habe ich mich nach diesen gerichtet, zum Beispiel in den 4/4-*Adagio* Sätzen.

ARTIKULATION

In seinem Autograph macht Mozart Silbenteilung − entsprechend seiner üblichen Praxis in Vokalmusik − durch Bindungen sowie durch Achtel- und Sechzehntelgruppen deutlich. In der vorliegenden Ausgabe werden solche Bindungen weggelassen. Man sollte jedoch bedenken, daß Bindebögen für Mozart sowohl Phrasierungen kennzeichnen, als auch dazu dienen, das Unterliegende zu verdeutlichen. Die gepaarten Noten in der Phrase "Quantus tremor est futurus" (Dies Irae, Takt 41 ff.) müssen daher sehr stark phrasiert werden, längere Melismen wie zum Beispiel im Domine Jesu (Takte 35-40) deuten eine ruhige gut ausgehaltene Linie an. Im Gegensatz dazu bindet Mozart die langen Melismen im Kyrie nicht und deutet daher eine artikuliertere Ausführung an. Die wenigen Bindungen in den Vokalteilen beschränken sich auf Stellen, an denen Mozarts Bindungsmuster nicht genau der Silbenteilung folgt. In den Süßmayr-Teilen (ab dem Sanctus) finden sich keine Vokalbindungen. Süßmayr ist in seinem Autograph weniger konsequent in der Hinzufügung von Bindungen. Wo jene nicht der Silbenteilung entsprechen, ist es kaum glaubwürdig, daß sie der Phrasierung dienen sollten.

DER BEZIFFERTE BASS

Mozart wollte zweifellos einen genau bezifferten Bass für das Requiem liefern, nach C.P.E. Bachs Motto "indessen muß dennoch das Nothwendige und Wesentliche nicht vergessen werden."[9] Er schrieb Bezifferungen für die ersten drei Teile (Introitus, Kyrie* und Dies Irae), für den zweiten Takt von Rex Tremendae, für Confutatis (ab Takt 26) und für Takte 21-28 des Domine Jesu. Diese Ziffern geben wertvolle Aufschlüsse über die Ergänzung der Orchestrierung, zum Beispiel für die Nonakkorde in Takt 28 von Domine Jesu, die Süßmayr nicht beachtete. Mozart bestimmte darüber hinaus Orgelbeteiligung im Recordare, Lacrimosa und Hostias, indem er 'organo e basso' vor das unterste Notensystem schrieb. Für das Tuba Mirum ist keine Orgelbeteiligung vorgesehen. Handelt es sich möglicherweise um ein Versehen? Wollte Mozart eventuell einen durchgehenden Orgelpart mit Ausnahme der "senza organo"-Teile? Er verlangt Orgel im Recordare, einem weiteren Solosatz ohne Bezifferungen. Heutige Ausführende sind jedoch vielleicht der Meinung, daß eine Bezifferung keine besondere Bereicherung für die beiden Sätze darstellt und sehen davon ab. Handelt es sich angesichts der Tatsache, daß das Recordare der einzige Satz ist, für den Mozart Orgel verlangt, dann jedoch keine weiteren Angaben macht, bei dem "organo e basso" vielleicht um einen Fehler?

Abgesehen davon, daß Süßmayr Mozarts Bezifferung kopiert, ergänzt er auch die Bezifferung zu Mozarts Fortführung des Lacrimosa, vervollständigt seine Bezifferung des Domine Jesu (mit Ausnahme der letzten sieben Takte) und trägt Bezifferungen für seine Versionen von Sanctus, Agnus Dei und, etwas sporadisch, Benedictus ein. Ich habe für meine Ergänzung, indem ich Mozarts vermutlichem Vorbild im Tuba Mirum folgte, keine Orgel im Benedictus benötigt, habe aber ansonsten Bezifferungen hinzugefügt (in dieser Vokalpartitur gibt es keine, aber sie sind in der vollständigen Ausgabe enthalten, die von Novello ausgeliehen werden kann). Ich habe auch einen Generalbaß für das ganze Werk mit Ausnahme des Tuba Mirum geschrieben (ebenfalls ausleihbar). Entsprechend zahlreichen modernen Ausgaben (zum Beispiel Bärenreiters Neue Mozart Ausgabe), habe ich Mozarts und Süßmayrs Ziffern ergänzt, indem ich die Bezifferung der ersten Ausgabe der Instrumentalteile des Requiems (Wien 1812) verwendete.

Ich habe meinen Generalbaß so einfach wie möglich gehalten, indem ich einer weiteren Anweisung C.P.E. Bachs folgte, wonach Continuobegleitung vor allem diskret[11] sein sollte. Bachs *Versuch über die wahre Art das Clavier zu spielen* enthält in dem Kapitel über Begleitung die beste zeitgenössische Anweisung für denjenigen, der seine eigene Version schaffen will. Mein Orgelteil sollte sowieso nur als Anregung betrachtet werden; je nach Instrument und verwendetem Register, Zahl der Ausführenden und Akustik der Kirche oder des Saals können

Noten weggenommen oder hinzugefügt werden, um ein besseres Gleichgewicht zu erzielen.

PRINZIPIEN DER NEUEN AUSGABE

Süßmayrs Arbeit am Mozartrequiem besteht aus zwei Teilen: der Vervollständigung des Instrumentalsatzes, für die Mozart schon einen vollständigen Entwurf der Vokalstimmen und Baßlinie bereitgestellt hatte, und die Kompositionsarbeit, die er mit dem Schreiben oder der Vervollständigung der anderen Teile ausführte. Während das Werk als Ganzes sich als eines von Mozarts Beliebtesten und Bewundertsten erwiesen hat, so war es seit seiner Veröffentlichung klar, daß es ihm gelegentlich an der Perfektion der Details mangelte, der geschmeidigen Handwerkskunst, dem einfallsreichen Verhältnis von untergeordnetem Material zum Ganzen, die so charakteristisch für Mozarts andere, reife Meisterwerke sind. Süßmayrs Orchestrierung, die oft sehr kunstgerecht, gelegentlich jedoch unbeholfen und selten einfallsreich ist, steht Mozarts Vision zwar nur selten im Weg, erhöht sie jedoch auch kaum. In jenen Teilen, für die Süßmayr sich verantwortlich erklärte, sind ernstere Mängel vorhanden: die nachlässige Qualität der Osanna-Fugen, die harmonische Stagnation in dem Hauptteil des Benedictus sind zwei solche Enttäuschungen. Dennoch betonen die Hauptideen all dieser Teile, ob sie von Mozart stammen oder von Süßmayr allein komponiert waren, sehr stark die Einheit und den Charakter des Werks. Die Frage, welche Teile dieser Sätze, falls überhaupt, von Mozart stammen könnten, ist sehr oft und mit sehr unterschiedlichen Schlußfolgerungen diskutiert worden, u.a. von Beyer[12], Blume[13], Handke[14], Marguerre[15], Maunder[16], Moseley und Wolff. Ich habe hier nicht vor, mich in die Diskussionen einzumischen, sage aber, daß es schwierig ist, eine Autorenschaft aufgrund stilistischer Merkmale nachzuweisen oder zu verwerfen. Süßmayrs Fertigstellung wird immer einen besonderen Platz haben, aufgrund ihrer langen Aufführungsgeschichte, und weil sie die einzige von einem Wiener Komponisten der 1790er Jahre ist. Darüber hinaus von einem, der Mozarts Absichten bestens kannte.

Jeder, der es sich heute zur Aufgabe macht, das Requiem fertigzustellen, sieht sich grundlegenden Problemen gegenüber. Man kann sich nicht vollständig auf Parallelen mit anderen Werken Mozarts verlassen. Dafür sorgen die ungewöhnliche Orchestrierung des Requiems und der Mangel an vergleichsweise großen geistlichen Werken aus seinen letzten Jahren. Legen wir Wert auf das intensive Leben und die Individualität von selbst untergeordneten Details in Mozarts Musik, so erweisen wir ihm keinen Dienst, wenn wir lediglich ausgesuchte

*Paul Moseley[10] wies kürzlich darauf hin, daß die Bezifferung im Kyrie ab Takt 20 (in unserer Ausgabe Takt 68) von Süßmayrs Hand stammt.

Einzelheiten aus anderen Stücken wiederholen. Obwohl ich keineswegs die Möglichkeiten von wirklich nützlichen Parallelen in anderen Stücken Mozarts ignoriert habe, habe ich versucht, mich auf allgemeinere Weise in die Position eines Wiener Komponisten aus Mozarts Zeit zu versetzen, der die große Anlage des Werks auf überzeugendste Art und Weise vervollständigen wollte. Ich begann das Lacrimosa, indem ich Joseph Eyblers Versuch einer Fortsetzung folgte und einen Satz komponierte, dessen Konstruktion der des Dies Irae am Beginn der Sequenz glich. Das Sanctus ist eine Bearbeitung der Version Süßmayrs. Für das Benedictus verwandte ich das thematische Hauptmaterial der traditionellen Fassung (der Beginn stammt sowieso von Mozart — er findet sich in KV 453b, dem Übungsbuch für Barbara Ployer[17]) und komponierte einen neuen Satz, indem ich zahlreichen Modellen und Hinweisen Mozarts folgte. Das Agnus Dei, das allgemein für den überzeugendsten der "Süßmayr" Sätze gehalten wird, habe ich bezüglich der vokalen und Bass-Teile bis zum letzten Teil beibehalten. Ich habe jedoch eine längere instrumentale Einleitung zum Lux Aeterna* hinzugefügt. Es erschien mir wichtig, die Atmosphäre und das Material des Introitus auf entschiedenere Weise wieder einzuführen. Für die fugalen Chöre zum "Amen" und "Osanna" habe ich vor allem die

fugalen Stücke im Requiem als Modelle verwendet, die von Mozart vervollständigt worden waren — das Kyrie und Quam Olim Abrahae-Teile sowie das Cum Sancto Spiritu der Messe in c-moll KV 427 und instrumentale Fugen wie jene in c-moll KV 426. Der Ausgangspunkt für das Amen war die kurze autographe Skizze, auf die oben verwiesen wird. Für das Osanna verwendete ich das Thema der Süßmayr-Version. Wenn das Amen und das erweiterte Osanna den anderen großangelegten Chorsätzen hinzugefügt werden, wird die chorische Voreingenommenheit des ganzen Werks mit seinen eindrucksvollen, absichtlich archaischen Kontrapunktmerkmalen sogar noch deutlicher.

In den vergangen Jahren[18] erschienen zahlreiche neue Versionen von Mozarts Requiem; jede hat einen anderen Schwerpunkt bezüglich der nötigsten "Verbesserungen". Diese Fassungen verdeutlichen das derzeitige große Interesse an Mozarts Musik und erscheinen mir als ein gutes Zeichen. Das Requiem ist schließlich das größte Werk Mozarts, für das es keine definitive Version gibt. Wir können sehr viel von ihm lernen und uns von ihm inspirieren lassen, wenn wir es aus verschiedenen Perspektiven sehen. Einige Aspekte von Mozarts Vision mögen durch eine Fertigstellung verdunkelt worden sein, während sie durch eine andere verbessert wurden. E.T.A. Hoffmann war sich 1814 schon sehr der Qualitäten des Requiems bewußt als er schrieb "[s]onst bleibt die Musik überall reiner Kultus, und nur als solcher ertönen die wunderbaren Akkorde, die von dem Jenseits sprechen, ja, die das Jenseits selbst sind, in ihrer eigentümlichen Würde und Kraft[19].

DUNCAN DRUCE, Holmbridge, Juni 1992.

*Dies bereitete Probleme mit der Taktnumerierung. In der Version Süßmayrs werden Agnus Dei und Communio zusammengezählt; für die neue Fertigstellung werden Agnus Dei und die ersten 6 Takte des Lux Aeterna getrennt numeriert, und treffen in Takt 53 wieder mit der Numerierung Süßmayrs "zusammen".

Anmerkungen

1) Niemetschek, Franz Xaver. *Leben des k.k. Kapellmeisters Wolfgang Gottlieb Mozart* (Prague 1798).
2) Rochlitz, Friedrich. 'Verbürgte Anekdoten aus Wolfgang Gottlieb Mozarts Leben', *Allgemeine Musikalische Zeitung*, Leipzig, Oct-Dec. 1798.
3) Herzog, Anton: *Wahre und ausführliche Geschichte des Requiem von W.A. Mozart.*
4) Veröffentlicht in der Einleitung (von Günther Brosche) zur Bärenreiter-Faksimileausgabe der Requiemhandschriften, Kassel 1990.
5) Brief an Maximilian Stadler datiert 14.3.1827. Bauer, A. und Deutsch, O.E. (Hgg.): *Mozart: Briefe und Aufzeichnungen*, Bd.4, S.491f, Bärenreiter 1963.
6) Erstmals veröffentlicht in Plath, W.: 'Über Skizzen zu Mozarts Requiem', *Bericht über den Internationalen Musikwissenschaftlichen Kongress, Kassel 1962*, S. 184ff., Kassel 1963.
7) Die beiden Bände sind nun auch als Faksimiles erhältlich (vgl. Anmerkung 4).
8) Wolff, C.: 'The Composition and Completion of Mozart's Requiem, 1791-2', *Mozart Studies*, Hrsg. Eisen, C., Clarendon Press, Oxford.
9) Bach, C.P.E.: *Versuch über die wahre Art das Clavier zu spielen* (2 Teile, Berlin 1753 und 1762, nachgedruckt 1780, 1787 und 1797).

10) Moseley, P.: 'Mozart's Requiem: A re-evaluation of the evidence', *Journal of the Royal Musical Association*, 114 (1989).
11) Bach, C.P.E., Ibid.
12) Einleitung zu *Mozart: Requiem*, Hrsg. Beyer, Franz; Zürich, Eulenberg, 1971, 1980.
13) Blume, F.: 'Requiem but no Peace', *The Musical Quarterly*, 17 (1961), S. 147ff.
14) Handke, R.: 'Zur Lösung der Benedictusfrage', *Mozarts Requiem, Zeitschrift für Musikwissenschaft*, 1 (1918), S. 108ff.
15) Marguerre, K.: 'Mozart und Süssmayr', *Mozart-Jahrbuch*, 1962-3, S.172ff.
16) Maunder, R.: *Mozart's Requiem: on preparing a new edition*, Clarendon Press, Oxford, 1988. Vgl. besonders S. 33ff.
17) Diese Ähnlichkeit wurde zuerst beobachtet von R. Lach in 'W.A. Mozart als Theoretiker', *Denkschriften der Akademie der Wissenschaften in Wien (philosophisch-historische Klasse)*, 61 (1918) 1 Abhandlung. Maunder gibt ebenfalls den Auszug aus KV 453b wieder (Ibid, S.48).
18) Zum Beispiel jene von Beyer (vgl. Anmerkung 12); Richard Maunder (Oxford University Press, 1988); H.C. Robbins Landon (1989); und Robert Levin (1991).
19) Charlton, David (Hrsg.): *E.T.A. Hoffmann's Musical Writings*, S.374f, Cambridge University Press, 1989.

I INTROITUS: REQUIEM

No. 1

*Mozart slurs Do - mi-ne

4

*Alto: Mozart slurs
do - na

II KYRIE

8

10

III SEQUENZ
Dies Irae

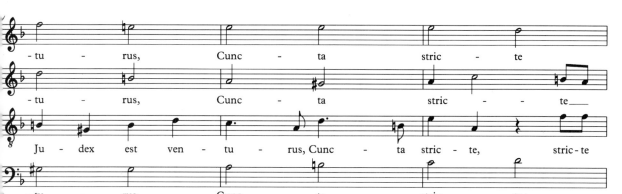

16

Quan - tus tre - mor_ est_ fu - tu - rus, Quan-do
Quan - tus tre - mor_ est_ fu - tu - rus, Quan-do
Quan - tus tre - mor_ est_ fu - tu - rus, Quan-do
tre - mor_ est_ fu - tu rus, Quan - tus tre - mor_ est_ fu - tu - rus, Quan-do

49

Ju - dex est ven - tu - rus, Cunc-ta stric - te dis - cus -
Ju - dex est ven - tu - rus, Cunc-ta stric - te dis - cus -
Ju - dex est ven - tu - rus, Cunc-ta stric - te dis - cus -
Ju - dex est ven - tu - rus, Cunc-ta stric - te dis - cus -

53

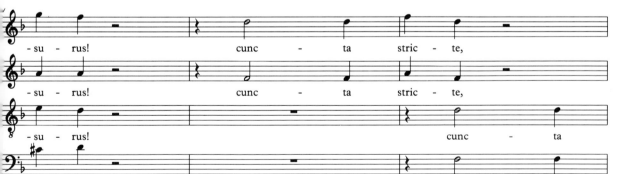

- su - rus! cunc - ta stric - te,
- su - rus! cunc - ta stric - te,
- su - rus! cunc - ta
- su - rus! [v] cunc - ta

56

59

62

65

No. 3

Tuba Mirum

20

22

No. 4

Rex Tremendae

25

26

No. 5

Recordare

30

Ante diem rationis, ante diem rationis, ante diem rationis.

Ingemisco

32

Mi - hi quo - que spem de - dis - ti, mi - hi quo - que spem de -

Mi - hi quo - que, mi - hi quo - que spem de - dis - ti, spem___ de -

- dis - ti, Mi - hi quo - que, mi - hi quo - que spem___ de -

Mi - hi quo - que spem de -

fp

87

- dis - ti.

- dis - ti. Pre - - ces me - - ae

- dis - ti.

- dis - ti. Pre - - ces me - ae___

Bt. Hns.
p

p

92

Sed___ tu bo - -

non sunt___ dig - nae:

Sed___ tu

___ non sunt dig - nae:

Vln.

tr

97

Vcl.

Confutatis Maledictis

38

*Soprano: Mozart slurs
(ac)-cli - nis

GGere

CHORUS: for Druce edition, turn to page 109

No. 7

Lacrimosa

42

* In bars 24-7 the alto and tenor parts have been altered to provide smoother part-writing. Süssmayr's original reads

On the first beat of bar 25 Süssmayr writes E♭ in the instrumental bass. This has been altered to G to fit the revised choral parts.

IV OFFERTORIUM
Domine Jesu

No. 8

* Tempo indication is Süssmayr's. By analogy with other Mozart movements with a similar rhythmic character, the editor would suggest a somewhat faster tempo (♩ = 100) of **Allegro moderato**.

46

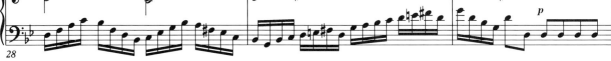

-prae-sen-tet e - - as in lu - cem sanc - tam,

sig - ni-fer sanc - tus Mi - cha-el Re - prae-sen-tet e - - as

Solo

Sed sig - ni-fer sanc - tus Mi - cha-el Re -

Solo

Sed

35

re - prae - sen-tet, re - prae-sen-tet e - as____

in lu - cem sanc - tam, re - prae-sen - tet, re-prae - sen-tet

-prae-sen-tet e - - as, re - prae - sen - tet e - as____

sig - ni-fer sanc - tus Mi - cha-el Re - prae-sen-tet e - as, re - prae-

39

____ in lu-cem sanc - tam:

e - as in lu-cem sanc - tam:

____ in__ lu - cem sanc - tam:

Tutti
[f]

-sen-tet e - as in lu-cem sanc - tam: Quam o-lim A - bra-hae

f

42

50

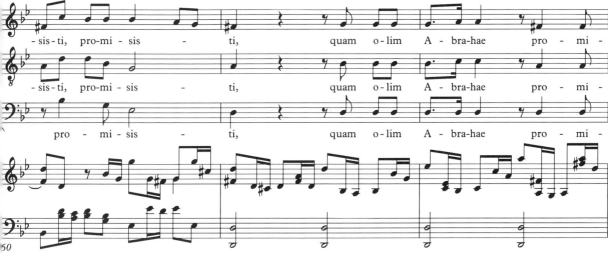

A - bra-hae pro - mi - sis - ti, quam o - lim A-bra-hae pro-mi - sis -

A - bra-hae pro - mi - sis - ti, quam o - lim A-bra-hae pro-mi - sis -

A - bra-hae pro - mi - sis - ti, quam o - lim A-bra-hae pro - mi - sis -

pro - mi-sis - ti, quam o-lim A-bra-hae pro-mi - sis-ti, pro-mi - sis -

72

- ti, et se - - - mi - ni e - - jus.

- ti, et se - mi-ni, se - mi - ni e - - jus.

- ti, et se - mi-ni, se - mi - ni e - - jus.

- ti, et se - mi-ni, se - mi - ni e - - jus.

75

No. 9

Hostias

* Süssmayr's tempo indication

ho - di - e me - mo - ri - am____ fa - ci - mus.

-mo - ri - am fa - - - ci - mus.

-mo - ri - am fa - - - ci - mus.

ho - di - e me - mo - ri - am fa - ci - mus.

41

p Fac e - as, Do - mi - ne, de mor - - te tran -

p Fac e - as, Do - mi - ne, de mor - te tran - si -

p Fac e - as, Do - mi - ne, de mor - - te tran -

p Fac e - as, Do - mi - ne, de mor - - te tran -

46

[**Andante con moto**] [♩ = 100]

-si - re ad vi - tam,

- re ad vi - tam,

-si - re ad vi - tam,

-si - re ad vi - tam,

[*f*]
Quam o-lim A - bra-hae

[**Andante con moto**] [♩ = 100]

f

51

58

60

A - bra-hae pro - mi - sis - ti, quam o - lim A-bra-hae pro-mi - sis -

A - bra-hae pro - mi - sis - ti, quam o - lim A-bra-hae pro-mi - sis -

A - bra-hae pro - mi - sis - ti, quam o - lim A-bra-hae pro-mi - sis -

pro - mi-sis - ti, quam o-lim A-bra-hae pro-mi - sis-ti, pro-mi - sis -

- ti, et se - - - mi-ni e - - jus.

- ti, et se - mi-ni, se - mi-ni e - - jus.

- ti, et se - mi-ni, se - mi-ni e - - jus.

- ti, et se - mi-ni, se - mi-ni e - - jus.

CHORUS: for Druce edition turn to page 130

V SANCTUS

No. 10

64

*Alto and L.H. accompaniment: an improvement on Süssmayr's phrase here might be

VI BENEDICTUS

No. 11

66

68

29

32

35

70

* B♭'s in Süssmayr's score, but G seems to be more likely his intention and makes a better melodic line.

VII AGNUS DEI

No. 12

74

VIII COMMUNIO
No. 13 Lux Aeterna

* This corresponds to bar 7 of COMMUNIO in the Druce version. Bar numbers in brackets are as for the Druce version.

*Alto: Süssmayr, following Mozart's example in the **Introit**, slurs

78

69(23)

72(26)

75(29)

lu - ce - at e - is, et lux per - pe - tu-a lu - ce - at e - is.

-pe - tu-a lu - ce - at e - is, et lux per - pe - tu-a lu - ce - at e - is.

-pe - tu-a lu - ce - at e - is, et lux per - pe - tu-a lu - ce - at e - is.

-pe - tu-a lu - ce - at e - is, et lux per - pe - tu-a lu - ce - at e - is.

78(32)

Allegro [♩ = 100]

Cum sanc-tis tu - is__ in__ ae - ter - - -

Cum sanc - tis tu - is in ae - ter - - -

Allegro [♩ = 100]

82(36)

Cum sanc - tis tu - is in ae - ter - -

- - num,

Cum sanc-tis tu - is__ in__ ae - ter - -

- - - num, cum sanc -

85(39)

88 (42)

91 (45)

94 (48)

84

MOZART

Requiem

K.626, completed by Duncan Druce
(see pp.1-11 for Introitus and Kyrie)

III SEQUENZ
Dies Irae

No. 2

88

41

45

49

53

Tuba Mirum

94

Rex Tremendae

No. 5

Recordare

111

116

121

126

Confutatis Maledictis

Andante [♩ = 76]

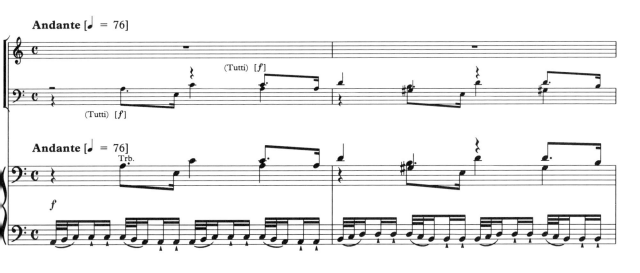

106

108

segue

No. 7

Lacrimosa

112

No. 7a

Amen

* Mozart's sketch (which consists of the four vocal parts only) breaks off here.

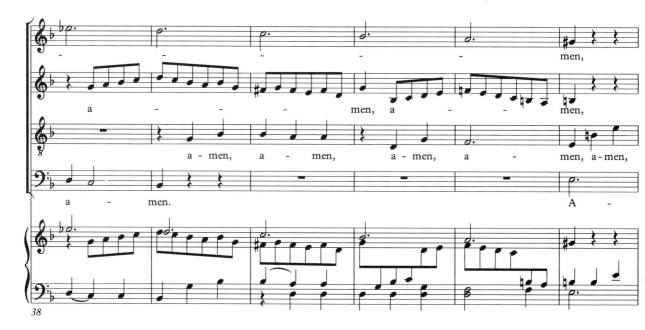

116

118

CHORUS: turn to page 45

IV OFFERTORIUM
Domine Jesu

No. 8

* Tempo indication as Süssmayr's. By analogy with other Mozart movements with a similar rhythmic character, the editor would suggest a somewhat faster tempo (♩ = 100) of **Allegro moderato**.

No. 9

Hostias

* Süssmayr's tempo indication

[Andante con moto] [♩ = 100]

[Andante con moto] [♩ = 100]

128

V SANCTUS

No. 10

132

VI BENEDICTUS

No. 11

The text under the solo vocal line reads: Be - ne-dic-tus qui ve-nit in no - mi-ne_

136

138

142

VII AGNUS DEI

No. 12

146

CHORUS/SOLI: turn to page 76

VIII COMMUNIO
Lux Aeterna

14 (60)

16 (62)

18 (64)

21 (67)

24 (70)

26 (72)

29 (75)

32 (78)

151

49(95)

52(98)

55(101)

58(104)

61 (107)

64 (110)

67 (113)

70 (116)

154

73 (119)

76 (122)

80 (126)

Adagio

Adagio

83 (129)

Printed in England by Caligraving Limited Thetford Norfolk

The New Novello Choral Edition

For 150 years Novello vocal scores have made a unique contribution to British choral singing, providing a mixture of accuracy, clarity, and competitive pricing that has been a benchmark for the rest of the field to emulate.

In recent years, however, ever-improving standards of musical scholarship and music engraving have led Novello to launch a series of completely new editions of the most popular choral works that will continue to set the standard for decades to come.

- **Prepared by respected scholars to the highest editorial standards.**

- **Full introductions in several languages give details of the historical background to the work and the editorial issues involved.**

- **Completely re-engraved music pages using the most sophisticated computer setting systems.**

- **Larger page-size for more generous spacing, yet retaining the layout of Novello's previous edition for ease of use in rehearsal, when both are often in use.**

All maintaining the Novello tradition of unbeatable value for money!

Currently available in the series:

Mendelssohn	*Elijah* ed. Michael Pilkington
Handel	*Messiah* ed. Watkins Shaw
Rossini	*Petite Messe Solenelle* (separate chorus part also available)
Mozart	*Requiem* ed. Duncan Druce (also including Druce's own completion)
Verdi	*Requiem* ed. Michael Pilkington
Handel	*Belshazzar* ed. Donald Burrows

The Handel works also form part of the ongoing *Novello Handel Edition*.